Fact Finders®

— DISGUSTING HISTORY —

The FOUL, FILTHY AMERICAN FRONTIER

THE DISGUSTING DETAILS ABOUT THE JOURNEY OUT WEST

by Heather E. Schwartz

Consultant:
Robert J. Moore Jr., PhD
Historian and Author
St. Louis, Missouri

CAPSTONE PRESS
a capstone imprint

Fact Finders is published by Capstone Press,
151 Good Counsel Drive, P.O. Box 669, Mankato, Minnesota 56002.
www.capstonepub.com

092010
005934WZS11

Library of Congress Cataloging-in-Publication Data
Schwartz, Heather E.
    The foul, filthy American frontier : the disgusting details about the journey out West / by Heather E.
Schwartz.
        p. cm. — (Fact finders. Disgusting history)
    Summary: "Describes disgusting details about daily life in the American frontier, including housing,
food, and sanitation" — Provided by publisher.
    Includes bibliographical references and index.
    ISBN 978-1-4296-3957-6 (library binding)
    ISBN 978-1-4296-6352-6 (paperback)
    1. Pioneers — West (U.S.) — History — 19th century — Juvenile literature. 2. Frontier and pioneer life —
West (U.S.) — Juvenile literature. 3. West (U.S.) — History — 19th century — Juvenile literature.
4. Overland journeys to the Pacific — Juvenile literature. I. Title. II. Series.
F596.S283 2010
978'.02 — dc22   2009031862

Editorial Credits

Christine Peterson, editor; Alison Thiele, designer; Wanda Winch, media researcher;
    Eric Manske, production specialist

Photo Credits

The Bancroft Library, U. of CA Berkeley, 20; Capstone Press, 4 (top), 19; CORBIS/James L. Amos, 22; Courtesy
Scotts Bluff National Monument, 4 (bottom), 9, 17; Getty Images Inc./Photodisc/The Palma Collection, cover;
Library of Congress, 5 (bottom), 10; NDSU-NDIRS, Fargo, Fred Hultstrand History in Pictures Collection,
25; North Wind Picture Archives, 6–7, 13, 14, 16, 26, 29; Nova Development Corporation, 5 (top, middle);
Shutterstock/akva, 9, 19 (design element); Shutterstock/freelanceartist, (design element throughout);
Shutterstock/Turi Tamas, (design element throughout); Shutterstock/Yuriy Chaban, 12; Wyoming Division of
Cultural Resources, 7 (bottom)

Primary source bibliography

Page 9 — from *Frontier Children* by Linda Peavy and Ursula Smith (Norman, Okla.: University
    of Oklahoma Press, 1999).
Page 19 — as published in *The Expedition of the Donner Party and its Tragic Fate* by Eliza P.
    Donner Houghton (Lincoln, Neb.: University of Nebraska Press, 1997).

TABLE OF CONTENTS

THE AMERICAN FRONTIER

1841–1866

OREGON CITY, OR.

SUTTER'S FORT

PACIFIC OCEAN

MAY 1804

Explorers Meriwether Lewis and William Clark begin their journey across America to explore the West.

AMERICAN FRONTIER BY THE NUMBERS

500,000 – people who followed trails to the Western United States, 1840–1860

20,000 – number of people who died on the way west

2,000 – miles settlers traveled to get from Missouri to California or Oregon

1,600 – average number of pounds carried by a single wagon, including food and belongings

170 – average number of days it took settlers to travel west

1841

Oregon Trail traffic by pioneer farmers begins with the Bidwell-Bartleson Party of 71 people.

1846

Trail traffic increases with the addition of Mormon pioneers seeking religious freedom in Utah.

JULY 27, 1836

FROM THE DIARY OF NARCISSA WHITMAN, ONE OF THE FIRST WHITE WOMEN TO SETTLE WEST OF THE ROCKY MOUNTAINS

"We have plenty of dried buffalo meat, which we have purchased from the Indians — and dry it is for me. It appears so filthy! I can scarcely eat it; but it keeps us alive, and we ought to be thankful for it."

NOVEMBER 2, 1846

PAGE 18

The Donner Party is trapped by a snowstorm in the Sierra Nevada mountains. They are not rescued until February 1847.

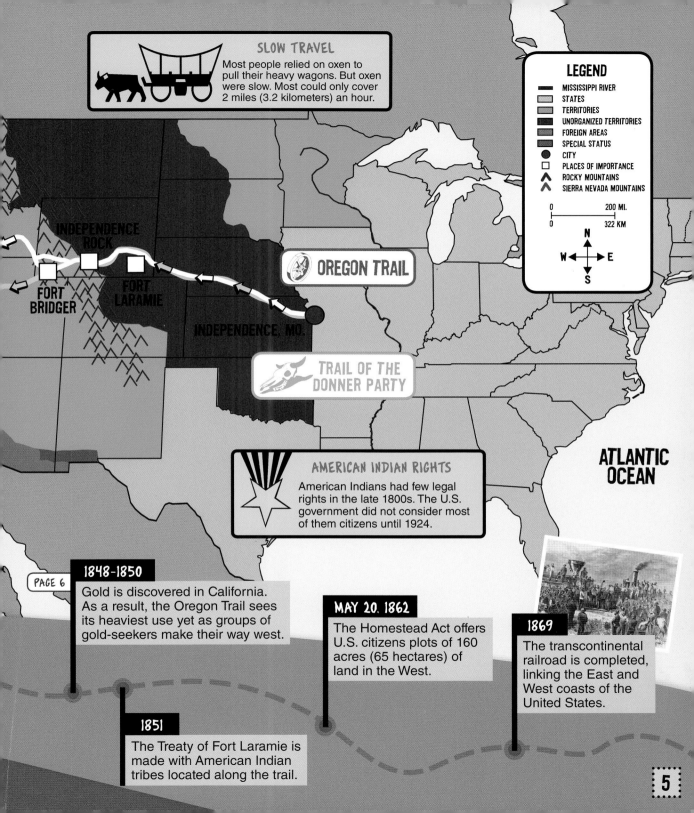

SLOW TRAVEL
Most people relied on oxen to pull their heavy wagons. But oxen were slow. Most could only cover 2 miles (3.2 kilometers) an hour.

PAGE 6

LEGEND

— MISSISSIPPI RIVER
☐ STATES
☐ TERRITORIES
■ UNORGANIZED TERRITORIES
☐ FOREIGN AREAS
☐ SPECIAL STATUS
● CITY
☐ PLACES OF IMPORTANCE
∧ ROCKY MOUNTAINS
∧ SIERRA NEVADA MOUNTAINS

0   200 MI.
0   322 KM

N
W — E
S

INDEPENDENCE ROCK

FORT BRIDGER

FORT LARAMIE

INDEPENDENCE, MO.

OREGON TRAIL

TRAIL OF THE DONNER PARTY

AMERICAN INDIAN RIGHTS
American Indians had few legal rights in the late 1800s. The U.S. government did not consider most of them citizens until 1924.

ATLANTIC OCEAN

1848-1850
Gold is discovered in California. As a result, the Oregon Trail sees its heaviest use yet as groups of gold-seekers make their way west.

MAY 20, 1862
The Homestead Act offers U.S. citizens plots of 160 acres (65 hectares) of land in the West.

1869
The transcontinental railroad is completed, linking the East and West coasts of the United States.

1851
The Treaty of Fort Laramie is made with American Indian tribes located along the trail.

THE JOURNEY BEGINS

In the mid-1800s, many Americans were restless. Farmers longed for more land. Others hoped to find riches during the California gold rush. Some people went west in search of religious or social freedoms. Hoping for a better life, thousands of families crammed covered wagons full of food and belongings. They set out across the American **frontier**.

No one expected an easy trip. But many people weren't well enough to handle the trip. Sick people walked or rode in wagons, hoping for better health out west. Pregnant women followed their husband's dreams. They suffered from nausea and tiredness. Many women gave birth along the way.

frontier: the territories of western North America in the 1800s unsettled by whites

pioneer: someone who explores an unknown territory or settles there

During the day the **pioneers** sweated under the hot sun. They endured dust storms and swarms of mosquitoes. At night temperatures fell. Thunderstorms pounded pioneers with rain and hail.

Pioneers had to keep moving. Any delays could cause them to run out of food or be trapped in the snowy mountains. Despite the bitter cold and blistering heat, pioneers pushed on toward a new start in the West.

INSIDE OF A COVERED WAGON

Pioneer families loaded wagons and animals with belongings for the trip out west.

TOUGHING IT OUT

Westward **caravans** traveled at a steady pace to reach their destinations. Most pioneers made the journey west on foot. Many of them were barefoot. Passengers in a covered wagon only added weight for tired oxen to pull. The wagon's rocking motion and musty smells often made riders sick.

Some caravans struggled more than others. Some groups followed risky shortcuts. These unproven paths were often covered with trees and brush. Groups lost valuable travel time moving boulders and clearing new trails.

Pioneers walked across deserts, pushed their wagons up mountains, and waded through muddy rivers. It wasn't long before their pants and skirts were torn and filthy with dirt. Some travelers didn't even have a change of clothes for the journey.

FOUL FACT

Some historians believe that one in 10 travelers died during the journey west on the Oregon Trail.

caravan: a group of covered wagons led by pioneers traveling together

Desert Crossing

We are traveling across a desert covered in prickly pears. My brothers and I don't wear shoes, and the prickly pear needles cut into our feet. It is our job to gather buffalo chips into a basket for building a fire later on. Each night, we are covered in dust. When the dry heat cracks and blisters our lips, we rub them with axle grease. Father says we will walk 15 miles each day.

Henry, age 10
May 1849

STOPS ALONG THE TRAIL

Each night, pioneers circled their wagons and made camp. But despite the open plains, travelers often found themselves surrounded by garbage left by other **emigrants**.

Travelers left behind rotting bodies of animals dead from starvation and exhaustion. Human and animal waste littered campsites. Empty supply bins and unwanted household items were scattered about. Heavy family **heirlooms** were tossed out.

Bathroom breaks were needed on the journey west. On the flat plains without a hill or tree in sight, no one had any real privacy. Men would use one side of the trail as a bathroom. Women would use the other side. Their long, full skirts provided some privacy during bathroom breaks on the trail.

emigrant: a person who leaves his or her own country or place of residence to settle elsewhere

heirloom: something important that is owned by a family member and handed down from one generation to the next

COOKING WITH DUNG

Before leaving home, pioneers packed enough flour, sugar, salt, meat, and other goods to last about seven months. Along the way they'd use the supplies to make meals of baked bread, pancakes, and fried meat.

But as the journey grew longer, the meals got worse. If people didn't plan carefully, their food would run out. With few options, some people killed and ate their pack mules to survive. People boiled and ate buffalo hides. When food was really scarce, pioneers dined on leftover flour bags, boiled shoe leather, and even leather pants.

No matter what was on the menu, cooking on the trail was a dirty job. Some pioneers cooked on cast iron wood stoves. But many cooked over an open campfire.

COOKING POT

Travelers often cooked fresh game over open fires.

Little wood was available on the plains. Most fires were built over a pile of weeds and buffalo chips. As a result, the food typically had a lasting smell of smoke and dung. Campfires flared and food burned easily in the wind. When it rained it was impossible to keep a fire lit. If emigrants couldn't cook, they might be stuck eating raw bacon until the sun came out again.

WATER WORRIES

Traveling on hot, dusty trails made the pioneers dry with thirst. Clean water was often hard to find on the way west. Pioneers had no choice but to drink water made dirty by human and animal waste. It was either drink the foul water or die of **dehydration**.

People also had to deal with the bitter-tasting **alkaline** water that was common along the trails. They disguised the taste by making coffee. But people had to be careful. Strong alkaline water could kill humans, oxen, and other animals. The water could cause internal burns, stomach pain, and fever. Some victims even vomited blood.

Dying of thirst was a real possibility on the hot plains. Water was also a problem in colder weather if a caravan became trapped.

> Livestock risked death without plenty of water on the trails.

dehydration: a life-threatening medical condition caused by a lack of water

alkaline: a strong chemical that dissolves in water and can burn your skin

FOUL FACT

Pioneers and livestock often drank water from the same containers.

DEADLY CONDITIONS

Every mile of the pioneers' journey seemed to hold new hardships. Wagons tipped over on steep mountain paths. Pioneers had to wade across swollen rivers. They risked drowning, losing their livestock or wagons, or sinking into hidden quicksand. Some pioneers and their livestock were swept away by raging rivers.

Pioneers struggled to get their wagons and livestock across mountain paths.

American Indians and pioneers sometimes joined together to hunt buffalo.

Emigrants also worried about running into American Indians. By the 1850s thousands of pioneers passed deadly diseases to Indian tribes. As more people came west, American Indians worried about losing their way of life. Some became angry. Some tribes attacked caravans in hopes of stopping settlers. But other American Indians acted as guides and traded goods with the pioneers.

THE DONNER PARTY

In May 1846, a group of 87 people and 23 wagons began the trip west. But it would be no ordinary journey. The Donner Party traveled slowly, took a risky shortcut, and crossed a stinging desert. In November 1846 a blizzard trapped the group in the Sierra Nevada mountains. Their supplies soon ran out. Some people starved to death. Others ate charred bones, twigs, bark, and leaves to survive.

A small group left camp to find help. They had little clothing or food. Soon the group was lost and out of food. Some starved to death. To survive the others ate the flesh of their dead companions.

Back at the campsite, the remaining members of the Donner Party ate mice and boiled tree branches. Still the months passed. Men, women, and children starved to death. The survivors began eating the dead. Only 46 members of the Donner Party survived. After the tragedy, volunteers organized West Coast Assistance and began searching for stranded emigrants each fall.

Desperate for Food

The little field mice that had crept into camp were caught then and used to ease the pangs of hunger. Also pieces of beef hide were cut into strips, singed, scraped, boiled to the consistency of glue, and swallowed with an effort; for no degree of hunger could make the saltless, sticky substance palatable. Marrowless bones which had already been boiled and scraped, were now burned and eaten, even the bark and twigs of pine were chewed in the vain effort to soothe the gnawings which made one cry for bread and meat.

Eliza P. Donner

DISEASE AND DEATH

Even when a wagon train was traveling on schedule, conditions were uncomfortable. Nearly every emigrant suffered from dysentery or diarrhea. Scurvy, caused by a lack of vitamin C, was also common. Victims had leg pain and bleeding gums. Cholera was one of the most feared diseases and also the most common. It caused vomiting and diarrhea and could kill within hours.

Pioneers couldn't do much to avoid disease or cure their ills. Sickness was treated with herbs, peppermint, rum, and whiskey. Sick travelers often became too weak to walk and had to ride in the cramped, stuffy wagon.

When disease didn't strike, accidents remained a serious threat. Buffalo stampedes trampled anyone in their paths. Rattlesnakes bit and poisoned their victims. People fell from moving wagons, sometimes getting crushed to death under the wheels.

PIONEER GRAVE

GRAVE SITUATIONS

Many pioneers didn't survive the trip west. When someone died, family members struggled with what to do with the body. The ground was too hard to dig a deep grave. There wasn't always time to build a coffin. Bodies were sometimes placed in a shallow grave without a coffin. Other bodies were simply covered with a pile of rocks.

When people knew they were dying on the trails, they worried about what would happen to their remains. They begged their families to protect them from grave robbers or hungry wolves.

Sometimes people carried a dead body with them rather than bury it in a spot they couldn't visit. Musty, strong-smelling **camphor** was sprinkled on the body and clothing to mask the scent of decay. One man traveling from Missouri to Oregon pickled a family member's body in a tub of whiskey for the trip.

camphor: a gummy, fragrant substance found in a camphor tree that is often used in medicine

FILTHY HOMESTEADS

Once pioneers arrived out west, their hard work wasn't over. They needed shelter. Settlers in Oregon and California built log cabins or lived in tents.

Rather than continue west, some settlers made homes on the Great Plains. On these grasslands, logs weren't easy to find. Settlers there created dugouts and built homes made of sod. Hay on the floor helped warm sod homes in winter, but it also attracted fleas. Snakes and mice lived in the walls. When a sod roof was dry, dirt would sprinkle into the house. In rainy weather, the roof would leak muddy water.

Without indoor plumbing, a pioneer family needed an outhouse, which would serve as a toilet. This small building had a bench inside. A hole in the bench opened over a deep pit dug into the ground. The outhouse could be smelly, so a small window was cut at the top of the door.

SOD HOUSE

Pioneer children pitched in to start new lives in the West. Both girls and boys plowed fields, cleaned chicken coops, milked cows, and trapped wild animals to eat. Dinner might include antelope, raccoon, or rabbit meat. Some children skinned their catches and sold the fur to earn money for their families.

Pioneers ate many meals of cornmeal mush. Leftover mush from one meal was often fried and served at another.

Pioneer women often had to hunt for and prepare food.

SEARCH FOR FOOD

The search for food didn't end once settlers arrived in the West. Men hunted wild game for food. But meat spoiled quickly on a hot day. Settlers smoked, dried, and salted meat to prevent rotting. The meat tasted good, but it was tough to chew. People often compared it to shoe leather.

Settlers knew they risked developing scurvy if they didn't eat fruits and vegetables. These foods were also preserved to last through the winter. Some settlers didn't have containers for storage, so they used old kerosene cans. The cans were reused until someone noticed the food inside tasted like tin or had turned black.

Drinking water was another priority. Some people collected rainwater in barrels and pans. Before drinking it they'd skim off the flies, mosquitoes, and dust that collected on top of the water. Others dug a well near their house. They had to choose the well site carefully. Otherwise water would be made dirty by human and animal waste.

NEW DANGERS

On the frontier, pioneer families continued to struggle. Great Plains settlers worried about prairie fires, tornadoes, and dust storms that filled the air with brown grit. During winter wild blizzards covered their small homes with snow and ice. Settlers strung ropes from the house to the barn, so no one would be lost in a blizzard.

On the plains and in the western states, mothers treated injuries and illnesses as best they could. They had no help from trained doctors. They tried to keep their children safe from wild animals like rattlesnakes and mountain lions. They feared attack by American Indians, although many Indians were friendly. Indians shared food, like a bread made with crickets and dried acorns.

Settlers struggled to build new communities on the rugged frontier. They built churches and one-room schools. But building materials weren't always available. Sometimes children learned their lessons in a boxcar, sheep wagon, tent, or chicken house.

Prairie fires threatened homes and crops.

With the journey behind them, the settlers could build new lives. Some stayed put. Many struck out again, moving farther and farther west. They were pioneers eager to explore new places and opportunities before settling down for good.

GLOSSARY

alkaline (AL-kuh-line) — a strong chemical that dissolves in water and can burn your skin

camphor (KAM-fuhr) — a gummy, fragrant substance found in the wood and bark of a camphor tree

caravan (KA-ruh-van) — a group of covered wagons led by pioneers traveling together

dehydration (dee-hy-DRAY-shuhn) — a life-threatening medical condition caused by a lack of water

dysentery (DI-sen-tayr-ee) — a serious infection of the intestines that can be deadly; dysentery is often caused by drinking contaminated water.

emigrant (EM-i-gruhnt) — a person who leaves his or her own country or place of residence to settle elsewhere

frontier (fruhn-TEER) — the territories of western North America in the 1800s unsettled by whites

heirloom (AIR-loom) — something important that is owned by a family member and handed down from one generation to the next

pioneer (pye-uh-NEER) — someone who explores an unknown territory or settles there

READ MORE

Friedman, Mel. *The Oregon Trail*. A True Book. New York: Children's Press, 2010.

Harkins, Susan Sales, and William H. Harkins. *The Donner Party*. What's So Great About? Hockessin, Del.: Mitchell Lane, 2009.

Lassieur, Allison. *Westward Expansion: An Interactive History Adventure*. You Choose Books. Mankato, Minn.: Capstone Press, 2008.

McCarthy, Pat. *Heading West: Life with the Pioneers, 21 Activities*. Chicago: Chicago Review Press, 2009.

INTERNET SITES

FactHound offers a safe, fun way to find Internet sites related to this book. All of the sites on FactHound have been researched by our staff.

Here's all you do:

Visit *www.facthound.com*

FactHound will fetch the best sites for you!

INDEX